ARTICULATION DRILL SKILLS

A bat on a ball.

A bug on a bird.

A baby on a boat.

A tub on a bus.

By Jean Gilliam DeGaetano
Illustrations by Kevin M. Newman

Great Ideas for Teaching, Inc. • P.O. Box 444 • Wrightsville Beach, NC 28480-0444

Copyright 2001 Great Ideas for Teaching, Inc.
All rights reserved. Printed in the U.S.A.
Published by Great Ideas for Teaching, Inc.
P.O. Box 444, Wrightsville Beach, NC 28480

Copies of all materials may be reproduced for classroom use and homework assignments. Copies may not be produced for entire school districts, used for commercial resale, stored in a retrieval system, or transmitted in any form; electronic, mechanical, recording, etc. without the permission from the publisher.

ISBN 1-886143-53-6

ARTICULATION DRILL SKILLS

By Jean Gilliam DeGaetano

This unit of 120 reproducible masters addresses 20 target sounds:

b, d, f, g, h, j, k, l, m, n, p, r, s, t, v, w, z, ch, sh, th

The practice sheets are designed for students who are able to produce the target sounds in the initial, medial and final positions of words and who are now ready to practice the target sounds in phrases. There are five worksheets per target sound.

Repetitious sound practice in short phrases is an important step in learning to habitually use the target sounds. If this step is mastered, the student can more easily be successful in using the target sounds in short sentences and relaxed conversation.

All the phrases are illustrated. No reading is required. The pictures are humorous and sometimes silly, making the activities fun to practice. The selection of pictured objects is appropriate for preschoolers through second grade.

The phrases should be said aloud very slowly until the target sound is consistently correct. The student should use a mirror if this assists them in the production of their target sound.

The professional should write how many times the phrases were practiced during the therapy session. If the phrases are to be practiced for homework, this should be written in the homework space. A parent letter is provided to send home with the practice sheets.

Suggestions for Use:

1. Use the selected worksheets for repetitious drill work.

2. Use the selected worksheets for assigned homework practice.

3. Make two copies of a selected worksheet. Cut the pictures apart. Play memory match-up games, saying the phrase as each match is made.

4. Make two copies of a selected worksheet. Cut the pictures apart. Play "Go Fish." The object of the game is to match alike pictures until all the pictures have been matched. The instructor should decide how many pictures should be used.

5. Play "Take Away." Cut the pictures apart. Put down three cards face up. Have the child turn around while a picture is removed. Then have the child guess which picture was removed, saying the phrase for that picture.

Date _____

To the Parents of _____:

Your child is beginning to work on the correct production of the _____ sound in short phrases.

The directions at the top of each page tell you how many times the phrases were practiced during the therapy session and how many times your child should practice the phrases for homework.

At this time, only be concerned with the correct production of the target sound on the worksheet. Errors may occur on other sounds not yet worked on in therapy.

Thank you for your cooperation and assistance at home.

Sincerely,

_____
Speech-Language Pathologist

Name: _____ b

The purpose of this activity is to provide repetitious practice of the target sound in the initial position. Say the phrase for each picture as many times as indicated.

In Class: _____   Homework: _____

A bug on a bear.

A bug on a bell.

A bug on a bike.

A bug on a bowl.

A bug on a boat.

A bug on a bus.

A bug on a bed.

A bug on a box.

A bug on a bird.

A bug on a bat.

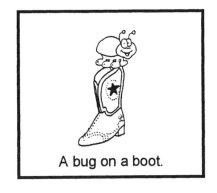
A bug on a boot.

A bug on a ball.

Great Ideas for Teaching, Inc.   b-1   ARTICULATION DRILL SKILLS

Name: _____ b

The purpose of this activity is to provide repetitious practice of the target sound in the initial position. Say the phrase for each picture as many times as indicated.

In Class: _____   Homework: _____

A bat on a bear.

A bat on a bell.

A bat on a bike.

A bat on a bowl.

A bat on a boat.

A bat on a bus.

A bat on a bed.

A bat on a box.

A bat on a bird.

A bat on a bat.

A bat on a boot.

A bat on a ball.

Great Ideas for Teaching, Inc.   ARTICULATION DRILL SKILLS

Name: _____ b

The purpose of this activity is to provide repetitious practice of the target sound in the initial position. Say the phrase for each picture as many times as indicated.

In Class: _____ Homework: _____

A bee on a bear.

A bee on a bell.

A bee on a bike.

A bee on a bowl.

A bee on a boat.

A bee on a bus.

A bee on a bed.

A bee on a box.

A bee on a bird.

A bee on a bat.

A bee on a boot.

A bee on a ball.

Great Ideas for Teaching, Inc.　　　　　ARTICULATION DRILL SKILLS

Name: _____ b

The purpose of this activity is to provide repetitious practice of the target sound in the initial and medial positions. Say the phrase for each picture as many times as indicated.

In Class: _____   Homework: _____

A baby on a bear.

A baby on a bell.

A baby on a bike.

A baby on a bowl.

A baby on a boat.

A baby on a bus.

A baby on a bed.

A baby on a box.

A baby on a bird.

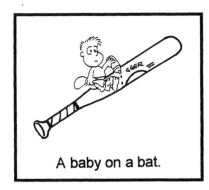
A baby on a bat.

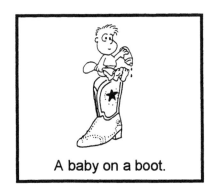
A baby on a boot.

A baby on a ball.

Great Ideas for Teaching, Inc.   ARTICULATION DRILL SKILLS

Name: _____ b

The purpose of this activity is to provide repetitious practice of the target sound in the initial and final positions. Say the phrase for each picture as many times as indicated.

In Class: _____ Homework: _____

A tub on a bear.

A tub on a bell.

A tub on a bike.

A tub on a bowl.

A tub on a boat.

A tub on a bus.

A tub on a bed.

A tub on a box.

A tub on a bird.

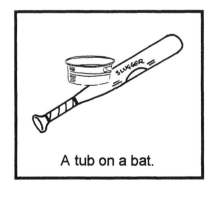
A tub on a bat.

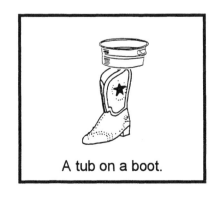
A tub on a boot.

A tub on a ball.

Great Ideas for Teaching, Inc.   ARTICULATION DRILL SKILLS

Name: _____ d

The purpose of this activity is to provide repetitious practice of the target sound in the initial position. Say the phrase for each picture as many times as indicated.

In Class: _____   Homework: _____

A doll on a doughnut.

A doll on a doctor.

A doll on a dog.

A doll on a doghouse.

A doll on a deer.

A doll on a door.

A doll on a duck.

A doll on a desk.

A doll on a doll.

A doll on a die.

A doll on some dishes.

A doll on a dart.

Great Ideas for Teaching, Inc.   ARTICULATION DRILL SKILLS

Name: _____ d

The purpose of this activity is to provide repetitious practice of the target sound in the initial position. Say the phrase for each picture as many times as indicated.

In Class: _____   Homework: _____

A duck on a doughnut.

A duck on a doctor.

A duck on a dog.

A duck on a doghouse.

A duck on a deer.

A duck on a door.

A duck on a duck.

A duck on a desk.

A duck on a doll.

A duck on a die.

A duck on some dishes.

A duck on a dart.

Name: _____ d

The purpose of this activity is to provide repetitious practice of the target sound in the initial position. Say the phrase for each picture as many times as indicated.

In Class: _____   Homework: _____

A dot on a doughnut.

A dot on a doctor.

A dot on a dog.

A dot on a doghouse.

A dot on a deer.

A dot on a door.

A dot on a duck.

A dot on a desk.

A dot on a doll.

A dot on a die.

A dot on some dishes.

A dot on a dart.

Great Ideas for Teaching, Inc.   d-3   ARTICULATION DRILL SKILLS

Name: _____ d

The purpose of this activity is to provide repetitious practice of the target sound in the initial and medial positions. Say the phrase for each picture as many times as indicated.

In Class: _____ Homework: _____

A panda on a doughnut.

A panda on a doctor.

A panda on a dog.

A panda on a doghouse.

A panda on a deer.

A panda on a door.

A panda on a duck.

A panda on a desk.

A panda on a doll.

A panda on a die.

A panda on some dishes.

A panda on a dart.

Great Ideas for Teaching, Inc.   d-4   ARTICULATION DRILL SKILLS

Name: _____ d

The purpose of this activity is to provide repetitious practice of the target sound in the initial and final positions. Say the phrase for each picture as many times as indicated.

In Class: _____ Homework: _____

A bed on a doughnut.

A bed on a doctor.

A bed on a dog.

A bed on a doghouse.

A bed on a deer.

A bed on a door.

A bed on a duck.

A bed on a desk.

A bed on a doll.

A bed on a die.

A bed on some dishes.

A bed on a dart.

Great Ideas for Teaching, Inc.   ARTICULATION DRILL SKILLS

Name: _____ f

The purpose of this activity is to provide repetitious practice of the target sound in the initial position. Say the phrase for each picture as many times as indicated.

In Class: _____   Homework: _____

A four on a fire engine.

A four on a fort.

A four on a fence.

A four on a fairy.

A four on a fish.

A four on a fan.

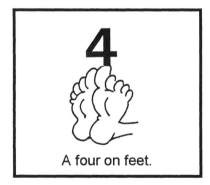
A four on feet.

A four on a fire.

A four on a fireman.

A four on a farmer.

A four on a fork.

A four on a fox.

Great Ideas for Teaching, Inc.　　　　ARTICULATION DRILL SKILLS

Name: _____ f

The purpose of this activity is to provide repetitious practice of the target sound in the initial position. Say the phrase for each picture as many times as indicated.

In Class: _____   Homework: _____

A fish on a fire engine.

A fish on a fort.

A fish on a fence.

A fish on a fairy.

A fish on a fish.

A fish on a fan.

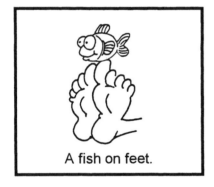
A fish on feet.

A fish on a fire.

A fish on a fireman.

A fish on a farmer.

A fish on a fork.

A fish on a fox.

Great Ideas for Teaching, Inc.　　　　　ARTICULATION DRILL SKILLS

Name: _____ f

The purpose of this activity is to provide repetitious practice of the target sound in the initial position. Say the phrase for each picture as many times as indicated.

In Class: _____   Homework: _____

A face on a fire engine.

A face on a fort.

A face on a fence.

A face on a fairy.

A face on a fish.

A face on a fan.

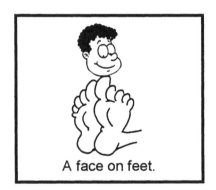
A face on feet.

A face on a fire.

A face on a fireman.

A face on a farmer.

A face on a fork.

A face on a fox.

Great Ideas for Teaching, Inc.　　　　f-3　　　　ARTICULATION DRILL SKILLS

Name: _____

f

The purpose of this activity is to provide repetitious practice of the target sound in the initial and medial positions. Say the phrase for each picture as many times as indicated.

In Class: _____   Homework: _____

Coffee on a fire engine.

Coffee on a fort.

Coffee on a fence.

Coffee on a fairy.

Coffee on a fish.

Coffee on a fan.

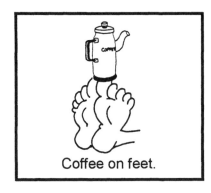
Coffee on feet.

Coffee on a fire.

Coffee on a fireman.

Coffee on a farmer.

Coffee on a fork.

Coffee on a fox.

Great Ideas for Teaching, Inc.   ARTICULATION DRILL SKILLS

Name: _____ f

The purpose of this activity is to provide repetitious practice of the target sound in the initial and final positions. Say the phrase for each picture as many times as indicated.

In Class: _____ Homework: _____

A leaf on a fire engine.

A leaf on a fort.

A leaf on a fence.

A leaf on a fairy.

A leaf on a fish.

A leaf on a fan.

A leaf on feet.

A leaf on a fire.

A leaf on a fireman.

A leaf on a farmer.

A leaf on a fork.

A leaf on a fox.

Great Ideas for Teaching, Inc. ARTICULATION DRILL SKILLS

Name: _____ g

The purpose of this activity is to provide repetitious practice of the target sound in the initial position. Say the phrase for each picture as many times as indicated.

In Class: _____ Homework: _____

A ghost on a gate.

A ghost on gum.

A ghost on a gorilla.

A ghost on a gift.

A ghost on a game.

A ghost on a golf bag.

A ghost on a guitar.

A ghost on a goalpost.

A ghost on a goat.

A ghost on a garage.

A ghost on a girl.

A ghost on a garbage can.

Great Ideas for Teaching, Inc.   g-1   ARTICULATION DRILL SKILLS

Name: _____ g

The purpose of this activity is to provide repetitious practice of the target sound in the initial position. Say the phrase for each picture as many times as indicated.

In Class: _____ Homework: _____

A goose on a gate.

A goose on gum.

A goose on a gorilla.

A goose on a gift.

A goose on a game.

A goose on a golf bag.

A goose on a guitar.

A goose on a goalpost.

A goose on a goat.

A goose on a garage.

A goose on a girl.

A goose on a garbage can.

Great Ideas for Teaching, Inc. ARTICULATION DRILL SKILLS

Name: _____ g

The purpose of this activity is to provide repetitious practice of the target sound in the initial position. Say the phrase for each picture as many times as indicated.

In Class: _____   Homework: _____

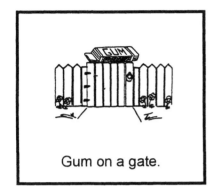
Gum on a gate.

Gum on gum.

Gum on a gorilla.

Gum on a gift.

Gum on a game.

Gum on a golf bag.

Gum on a guitar.

Gum on a goalpost.

Gum on a goat.

Gum on a garage.

Gum on a girl.

Gum on a garbage can.

Great Ideas for Teaching, Inc.   ARTICULATION DRILL SKILLS

Name: _____ g

The purpose of this activity is to provide repetitious practice of the target sound in the initial, medial and final positions. Say the phrase for each picture as many times as indicated.

In Class: _____   Homework: _____

A tiger on a gate.

A tiger on gum.

A tiger on a gorilla.

A tiger on a gift.

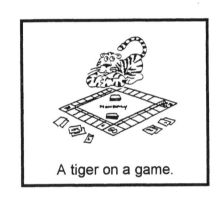
A tiger on a game.

A tiger on a golf bag.

A tiger on guitar.

A tiger on a goalpost.

A tiger on a goat.

A tiger on a garage.

A tiger on a girl.

A tiger on a garbage can.

Great Ideas for Teaching, Inc.　　　　g-4　　　　ARTICULATION DRILL SKILLS

Name: _____ g

The purpose of this activity is to provide repetitious practice of the target sound in the initial and final positions. Say the phrase for each picture as many times as indicated.

In Class: _____   Homework: _____

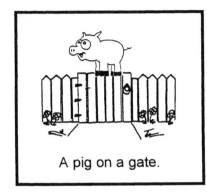
A pig on a gate.

A pig on gum.

A pig on a gorilla.

A pig on a gift.

A pig on a game.

A pig on a golf bag.

A pig on guitar.

A pig on a goalpost.

A pig on a goat.

A pig on a garage.

A pig on a girl.

A pig on a garbage can.

Great Ideas for Teaching, Inc.   ARTICULATION DRILL SKILLS

Name: _____ h

The purpose of this activity is to provide repetitious practice of the target sound in the initial position. Say the phrase for each picture as many times as indicated.

In Class: _____ Homework: _____

A hook on a hamburger.

A hook on a hoe.

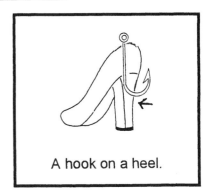
A hook on a heel.

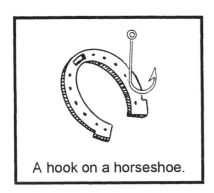
A hook on a horseshoe.

A hook on a hose.

A hook on a horn.

A hook on a horse.

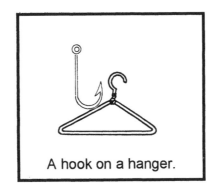
A hook on a hanger.

A hook on a helmet.

A hook on a hammer.

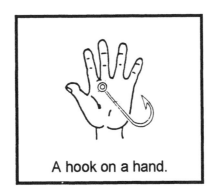
A hook on a hand.

A hook on a house.

Great Ideas for Teaching, Inc.　　ARTICULATION DRILL SKILLS

Name: _____ h

The purpose of this activity is to provide repetitious practice of the target sound in the initial position. Say the phrase for each picture as many times as indicated.

In Class: _____   Homework: _____

A heart on a hamburger.

A heart on a hoe.

A heart on a heel.

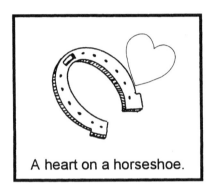
A heart on a horseshoe.

A heart on a hose.

A heart on a horn.

A heart on a horse.

A heart on a hanger.

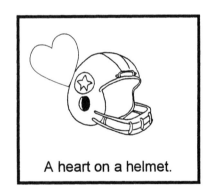
A heart on a helmet.

A heart on a hammer.

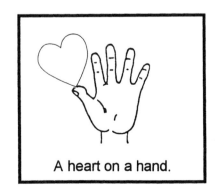
A heart on a hand.

A heart on a house.

Great Ideas for Teaching, Inc.   ARTICULATION DRILL SKILLS

Name: _____ h

The purpose of this activity is to provide repetitious practice of the target sound in the initial position. Say the phrase for each picture as many times as indicated.

In Class: _____ Homework: _____

A hat on a hamburger.

A hat on a hoe.

A hat on a heel.

A hat on a horseshoe.

A hat on a hose.

A hat on a horn.

A hat on a horse.

A hat on a hanger.

A hat on a helmet.

A hat on a hammer.

A hat on a hand.

A hat on a house.

Great Ideas for Teaching, Inc.   ARTICULATION DRILL SKILLS

Name: _____ h

The purpose of this activity is to provide repetitious practice of the target sound in the initial and medial positions. Say the phrase for each picture as many times as indicated.

In Class: _____   Homework: _____

A doghouse on a hamburger.

A doghouse on a hoe.

A doghouse on a heel.

A doghouse on a horseshoe.

A doghouse on a hose.

A doghouse on a horn.

A doghouse on a horse.

A doghouse on a hanger.

A doghouse on a helmet.

A doghouse on a hammer.

A doghouse on a hand.

A doghouse on a house.

Great Ideas for Teaching, Inc.   h-4   ARTICULATION DRILL SKILLS

Name: _____ h

The purpose of this activity is to provide repetitious practice of the target sound in the initial and medial positions. Say the phrase for each picture as many times as indicated.

In Class: _____   Homework: _____

A birdhouse on a hamburger.

A birdhouse on a hoe.

A birdhouse on a heel.

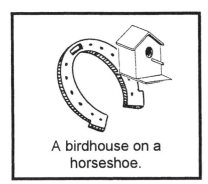
A birdhouse on a horseshoe.

A birdhouse on a hose.

A birdhouse on a horn.

A birdhouse on a horse.

A birdhouse on a hanger.

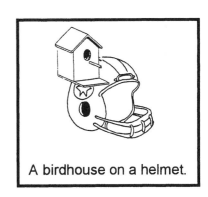
A birdhouse on a helmet.

A birdhouse on a hammer.

A birdhouse on a hand.

A birdhouse on a house.

Great Ideas for Teaching, Inc.   ARTICULATION DRILL SKILLS

Name: _____ **j**

The purpose of this activity is to provide repetitious practice of the target sound in the initial (and one final) position. Say the phrase for each picture as many times as indicated.

In Class: _____ Homework: _____

A jack-o'-lantern on a jar.

A jack-o'-lantern on a judge.

A jack-o'-lantern on a giraffe.

A jack-o'-lantern on a jeep.

A jack-o'-lantern on juice.

A jack-o'-lantern on a jack-in-the-box.

A jack-o'-lantern on a jug.

A jack-o'-lantern on a jacket.

A jack-o'-lantern on jelly beans.

A jack-o'-lantern on a juggler.

A jack-o'-lantern on a jail.

A jack-o'-lantern on a jump rope.

Great Ideas for Teaching, Inc.　　　j-1　　　ARTICULATION DRILL SKILLS

Name: _____ j

The purpose of this activity is to provide repetitious practice of the target sound in the initial (and one final) position. Say the phrase for each picture as many times as indicated.

In Class: _____   Homework: _____

A jar on a jar.

A jar on a judge.

A jar on a giraffe.

A jar on a jeep.

A jar on juice.

A jar on a jack-in-the-box.

A jar on a jug.

A jar on a jacket.

A jar on jelly beans.

A jar on a juggler.

A jar on a jail.

A jar on a jump rope.

Great Ideas for Teaching, Inc.   ARTICULATION DRILL SKILLS

Name: _____ j

The purpose of this activity is to provide repetitious practice of the target sound in the initial (and one final) position. Say the phrase for each picture as many times as indicated.

In Class: _____   Homework: _____

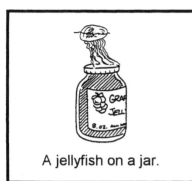
A jellyfish on a jar.

A jellyfish on a judge.

A jellyfish on a giraffe.

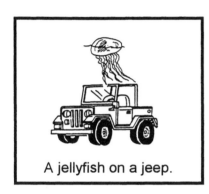
A jellyfish on a jeep.

A jellyfish on juice.

A jellyfish on a jack-in-the-box.

A jellyfish on a jug.

A jellyfish on a jacket.

A jellyfish on jelly beans.

A jellyfish on a juggler.

A jellyfish on a jail.

A jellyfish on a jump rope.

Great Ideas for Teaching, Inc.   ARTICULATION DRILL SKILLS

Name: _____ j

The purpose of this activity is to provide repetitious practice of the target sound in the initial, medial and final positions. Say the phrase for each picture as many times as indicated.

In Class: _____   Homework: _____

 An angel on a jar.	 An angel on a judge.	 An angel on a giraffe.
 An angel on a jeep.	 An angel on juice.	 An angel on a jack-in-the-box.
 An angel on a jug.	 An angel on a jacket.	 An angel on jelly beans.
 An angel on a juggler.	 An angel on a jail.	 An angel on a jump rope.

Great Ideas for Teaching, Inc.   ARTICULATION DRILL SKILLS

Name: _____ j

The purpose of this activity is to provide repetitious practice of the target sound in the initial, medial and final positions. Say the phrase for each picture as many times as indicated.

In Class: _____ Homework: _____

A cage on a jar.

A cage on a judge.

A cage on a giraffe.

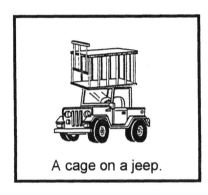
A cage on a jeep.

A cage on juice.

A cage on a jack-in-the-box.

A cage on a jug.

A cage on a jacket.

A cage on jelly beans.

A cage on a juggler.

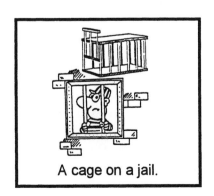
A cage on a jail.

A cage on a jump rope.

Great Ideas for Teaching, Inc. ARTICULATION DRILL SKILLS

Name: _____ k,c

The purpose of this activity is to provide repetitious practice of the target sound in the initial (and one final) position. Say the phrase for each picture as many times as indicated.

In Class: _____   Homework: _____

A cap on a king.

A cap on a car.

A cap on a key.

A cap on a cart.

A cap on a candle.

A cap on a camel.

A cap on a cake.

A cap on a coat.

A cap on a can.

A cap on a camera.

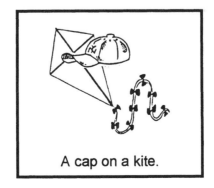
A cap on a kite.

A cap on corn.

Great Ideas for Teaching, Inc.   ARTICULATION DRILL SKILLS

Name: _____ k,c

The purpose of this activity is to provide repetitious practice of the target sound in the initial (and one final) position. Say the phrase for each picture as many times as indicated.

In Class: _____   Homework: _____

A cat on a king.

A cat on a car.

A cat on a key.

A cat on a cart.

A cat on a candle.

A cat on a camel.

A cat on a cake.

A cat on a coat.

A cat on a can.

A cat on a camera.

A cat on a kite.

A cat on corn.

Great Ideas for Teaching, Inc.   ARTICULATION DRILL SKILLS

Name: _____ k,c

The purpose of this activity is to provide repetitious practice of the target sound in the initial (and one final) position. Say the phrase for each picture as many times as indicated.

In Class: _____   Homework: _____

 A comb on a king.	 A comb on a car.	 A comb on a key.
 A comb on a cart.	 A comb on a candle.	 A comb on a camel.
 A comb on a cake.	 A comb on a coat.	 A comb on a can.
 A comb on a camera.	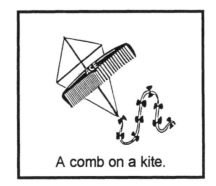 A comb on a kite.	 A comb on corn.

Great Ideas for Teaching, Inc.   k,c-3   ARTICULATION DRILL SKILLS

Name: _____ k,c

The purpose of this activity is to provide repetitious practice of the target sound in the initial, final and medial positions. Say the phrase for each picture as many times as indicated.

In Class: _____ Homework: _____

A turkey on a king.

A turkey on a car.

A turkey on a key.

A turkey on a cart.

A turkey on a candle.

A turkey on a camel.

A turkey on a cake.

A turkey on a coat.

A turkey on a can.

A turkey on a camera.

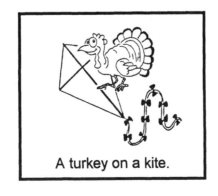
A turkey on a kite.

A turkey on corn.

Great Ideas for Teaching, Inc. k,c-4 ARTICULATION DRILL SKILLS

Name: _____ k,c

The purpose of this activity is to provide repetitious practice of the target sound in the initial and final positions. Say the phrase for each picture as many times as indicated.

In Class: _____ Homework: _____

A book on a king.

A book on a car.

A book on a key.

A book on a cart.

A book on a candle.

A book on a camel.

A book on a cake.

A book on a coat.

A book on a can.

A book on a camera.

A book on a kite.

A book on corn.

Name: _____ l

The purpose of this activity is to provide repetitious practice of the target sound in the initial position. Say the phrase for each picture as many times as indicated.

In Class: _____   Homework: _____

A leaf on lightning.

A leaf on a ladder.

A leaf on a log.

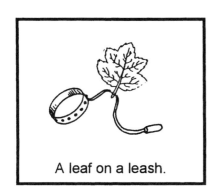
A leaf on a leash.

A leaf on a lemon.

A leaf on a lion.

A leaf on a lid.

A leaf on a leg.

A leaf on a lamp.

A leaf on a letter.

A leaf on a lock.

A leaf on a lunchbox.

Great Ideas for Teaching, Inc.   l-1   ARTICULATION DRILL SKILLS

Name: _____

The purpose of this activity is to provide repetitious practice of the target sound in the initial position. Say the phrase for each picture as many times as indicated.

In Class: _____ Homework: _____

A ladybug on lightning.

A ladybug on a ladder.

A ladybug on a log.

A ladybug on a leash.

A ladybug on a lemon.

A ladybug on a lion.

A ladybug on a lid.

A ladybug on a leg.

A ladybug on a lamp.

A ladybug on a letter.

A ladybug on a lock.

A ladybug on a lunchbox.

Name: _____ I

The purpose of this activity is to provide repetitious practice of the target sound in the initial and medial positions. Say the phrase for each picture as many times as indicated.

In Class: _____   Homework: _____

A lollipop on lightning.

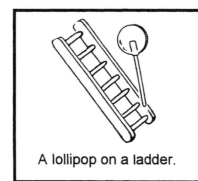
A lollipop on a ladder.

A lollipop on a log.

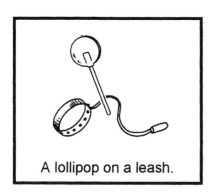
A lollipop on a leash.

A lollipop on a lemon.

A lollipop on a lion.

A lollipop on a lid.

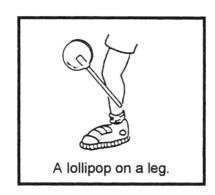
A lollipop on a leg.

A lollipop on a lamp.

A lollipop on a letter.

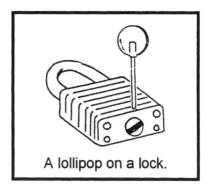
A lollipop on a lock.

A lollipop on a lunchbox.

Great Ideas for Teaching, Inc.   I-3   ARTICULATION DRILL SKILLS

Name: _____

The purpose of this activity is to provide repetitious practice of the target sound in the initial and medial positions. Say the phrase for each picture as many times as indicated.

In Class: _____ Homework: _____

A balloon on lightning.

A balloon on a ladder.

A balloon on a log.

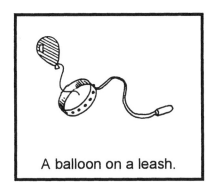
A balloon on a leash.

A balloon on a lemon.

A balloon on a lion.

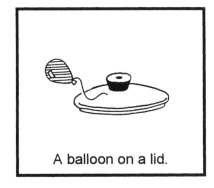
A balloon on a lid.

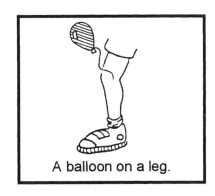
A balloon on a leg.

A balloon on a lamp.

A balloon on a letter.

A balloon on a lock.

A balloon on a lunchbox.

Name: _____ l

The purpose of this activity is to provide repetitious practice of the target sound in the initial and final positions. Say the phrase for each picture as many times as indicated.

In Class: _____ Homework: _____

A bell on lightning.

A bell on a ladder.

A bell on a log.

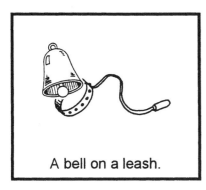
A bell on a leash.

A bell on a lemon.

A bell on a lion.

A bell on a lid.

A bell on a leg.

A bell on a lamp.

A bell on a letter.

A bell on a lock.

A bell on a lunchbox.

Great Ideas for Teaching, Inc.   ARTICULATION DRILL SKILLS

Name: _____

The purpose of this activity is to provide repetitious practice of the target sound in the initial position. Say the phrase for each picture as many times as indicated.

In Class: _____   Homework: _____

A mitten on a man.

A mitten on a mat.

A mitten on milk.

A mitten on money.

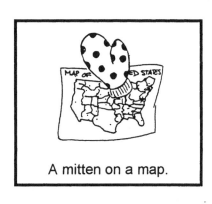
A mitten on a map.

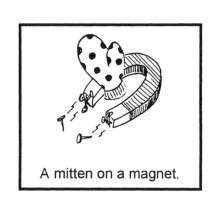
A mitten on a magnet.

A mitten on a monkey.

A mitten on a mitt.

A mitten on a mop.

A mitten on the moon.

A mitten on a mirror.

A mitten on some matches.

Great Ideas for Teaching, Inc.   ARTICULATION DRILL SKILLS

Name: _____ m

The purpose of this activity is to provide repetitious practice of the target sound in the initial position. Say the phrase for each picture as many times as indicated.

In Class: _____   Homework: _____

An "m" on a man.

An "m" on a mat.

An "m" on milk.

An "m" on money.

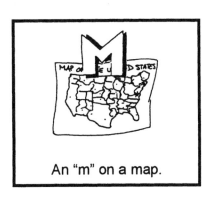
An "m" on a map.

An "m" on a magnet.

An "m" on a monkey.

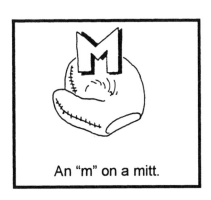
An "m" on a mitt.

An "m" on a mop.

An "m" on the moon.

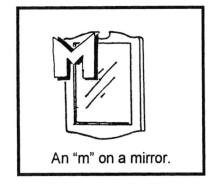
An "m" on a mirror.

An "m" on some matches.

Great Ideas for Teaching, Inc.   ARTICULATION DRILL SKILLS

Name: _____   m

The purpose of this activity is to provide repetitious practice of the target sound in the initial position. Say the phrase for each picture as many times as indicated.

In Class: _____   Homework: _____

A mouse on a man.

A mouse on a mat.

A mouse on milk.

A mouse on money.

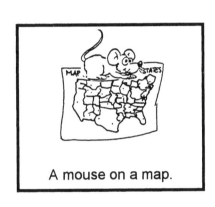
A mouse on a map.

A mouse on a magnet.

A mouse on a monkey.

A mouse on a mitt.

A mouse on a mop.

A mouse on the moon.

A mouse on a mirror.

A mouse on some matches.

Great Ideas for Teaching, Inc.   ARTICULATION DRILL SKILLS

Name: _____ m

The purpose of this activity is to provide repetitious practice of the target sound in the initial and medial positions. Say the phrase for each picture as many times as indicated.

In Class: _____ Homework: _____

A hammer on a man.

A hammer on a mat.

A hammer on milk.

A hammer on money.

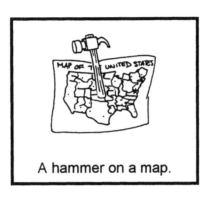
A hammer on a map.

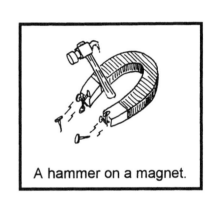
A hammer on a magnet.

A hammer on a monkey.

A hammer on a mitt.

A hammer on a mop.

A hammer on the moon.

A hammer on a mirror.

A hammer on some matches.

Great Ideas for Teaching, Inc. m-4 ARTICULATION DRILL SKILLS

Name: _____ m

The purpose of this activity is to provide repetitious practice of the target sound in the initial and final positions. Say the phrase for each picture as many times as indicated.

In Class: _____ Homework: _____

A ham on a man.

A ham on a mat.

A ham on milk.

A ham on money.

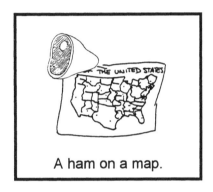
A ham on a map.

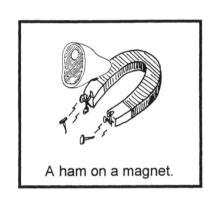
A ham on a magnet.

A ham on a monkey.

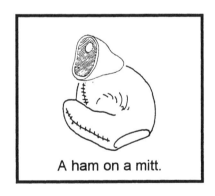
A ham on a mitt.

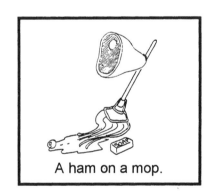
A ham on a mop.

A ham on the moon.

A ham on a mirror.

A ham on some matches.

Great Ideas for Teaching, Inc. m-5 ARTICULATION DRILL SKILLS

Name: _____ n

The purpose of this activity is to provide repetitious practice of the target sound in the initial position. Say the phrase for each picture as many times as indicated.

In Class: _____ Homework: _____

A nail on a nurse.

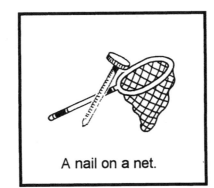
A nail on a net.

A nail on a nose

A nail on a knot.

A nail on a newspaper.

A nail on a nest.

A nail on numbers.

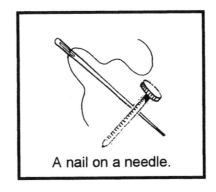
A nail on a needle.

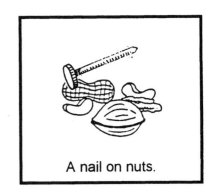
A nail on nuts.

A nail on a notebook.

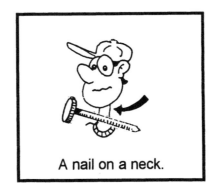
A nail on a neck.

A nail on a knee.

Great Ideas for Teaching, Inc. n-1 ARTICULATION DRILL SKILLS

Name: _____   **n**

The purpose of this activity is to provide repetitious practice of the target sound in the initial position. Say the phrase for each picture as many times as indicated.

In Class: _____   Homework: _____

A nine on a nurse.

A nine on a net.

A nine on a nose

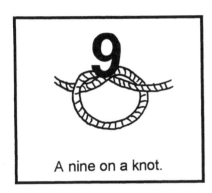
A nine on a knot.

A nine on a newspaper.

A nine on a nest.

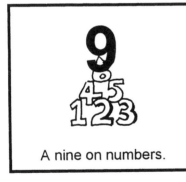
A nine on numbers.

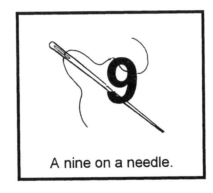
A nine on a needle.

A nine on nuts.

A nine on a notebook.

A nine on a neck.

A nine on a knee.

Great Ideas for Teaching, Inc.   ARTICULATION DRILL SKILLS

Name: _____ n

The purpose of this activity is to provide repetitious practice of the target sound in the initial position. Say the phrase for each picture as many times as indicated.

In Class: _____ Homework: _____

A net on a nurse.

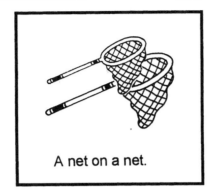
A net on a net.

A net on a nose

A net on a knot.

A net on a newspaper.

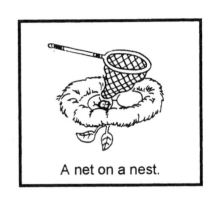
A net on a nest.

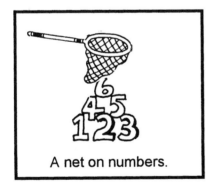
A net on numbers.

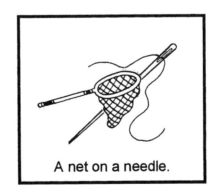
A net on a needle.

A net on nuts.

A net on a notebook.

A net on a neck.

A net on a knee.

Great Ideas for Teaching, Inc. ARTICULATION DRILL SKILLS

Name: _____ n

The purpose of this activity is to provide repetitious practice of the target sound in the initial and medial positions. Say the phrase for each picture as many times as indicated.

In Class: _____ Homework: _____

A pony on a nurse.

A pony on a net.

A pony on a nose

A pony on a knot.

A pony on a newspaper.

A pony on a nest.

A pony on numbers.

A pony on a needle.

A pony on nuts.

A pony on a notebook.

A pony on a neck.

A pony on a knee.

Great Ideas for Teaching, Inc.　　　ARTICULATION DRILL SKILLS

Name: _____ **n**

The purpose of this activity is to provide repetitious practice of the target sound in the initial and final positions. Say the phrase for each picture as many times as indicated.

In Class: _____ Homework: _____

A can on a nurse.

A can on a net.

A can on a nose

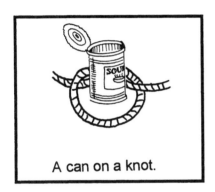
A can on a knot.

A can on a newspaper.

A can on a nest.

A can on numbers.

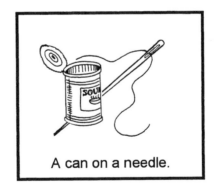
A can on a needle.

A can on nuts.

A can on a notebook.

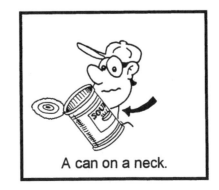
A can on a neck.

A can on a knee.

Great Ideas for Teaching, Inc. ARTICULATION DRILL SKILLS

Name: _____ p

The purpose of this activity is to provide repetitious practice of the target sound in the initial position. Say the phrase for each picture as many times as indicated.

In Class: _____   Homework: _____

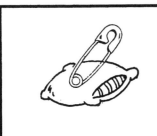
A pin on a pillow.

A pin on some pie.

A pin on a pig

A pin on paint.

A pin on a parrot.

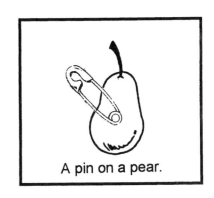
A pin on a pear.

A pin on a pen.

A pin on a pan.

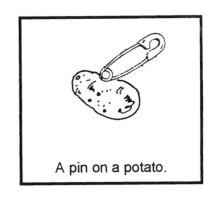
A pin on a potato.

A pin on a pencil.

A pin on a pail.

A pin on a painter.

Great Ideas for Teaching, Inc.   ARTICULATION DRILL SKILLS

Name: _____ p

The purpose of this activity is to provide repetitious practice of the target sound in the initial position. Say the phrase for each picture as many times as indicated.

In Class: _____ Homework: _____

A pear on a pillow.

A pear on some pie.

A pear on a pig

A pear on paint.

A pear on a parrot.

A pear on a pear.

A pear on a pen.

A pear on a pan.

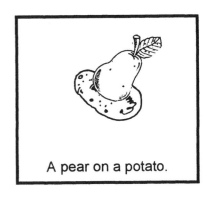
A pear on a potato.

A pear on a pencil.

A pear on a pail.

A pear on a painter.

Great Ideas for Teaching, Inc. ARTICULATION DRILL SKILLS

Name: _____ p

The purpose of this activity is to provide repetitious practice of the target sound in the initial position. Say the phrase for each picture as many times as indicated.

In Class: _____   Homework: _____

A penguin on a pillow.

A penguin on some pie.

A penguin on a pig

A penguin on paint.

A penguin on a parrot.

A penguin on pear.

A penguin on a pen.

A penguin on a pan.

A penguin on a potato.

A penguin on a pencil.

A penguin on a pail.

A penguin on a painter.

Great Ideas for Teaching, Inc.   ARTICULATION DRILL SKILLS

Name: _____ p

The purpose of this activity is to provide repetitious practice of the target sound in the initial and medial positions. Say the phrase for each picture as many times as indicated.

In Class: _____   Homework: _____

A puppy on a pillow.

A puppy on some pie.

A puppy on a pig

A puppy on paint.

A puppy on a parrot.

A puppy on a pear.

A puppy on a pen.

A puppy on a pan.

A puppy on a potato.

A puppy on a pencil.

A puppy on a pail.

A puppy on a painter.

Great Ideas for Teaching, Inc.   p-4   ARTICULATION DRILL SKILLS

Name: _____   p

The purpose of this activity is to provide repetitious practice of the target sound in the initial and final positions. Say the phrase for each picture as many times as indicated.

In Class: _____   Homework: _____

 A cup on a pillow.	 A cup on some pie.	 A cup on a pig
 A cup on paint.	 A cup on a parrot.	 A cup on a pear.
 A cup on a pen.	 A cup on a pan.	 A cup on a potato.
 A cup on a pencil.	 A cup on a pail.	 A cup on a painter.

Great Ideas for Teaching, Inc.   ARTICULATION DRILL SKILLS

Name: _____ r

The purpose of this activity is to provide repetitious practice of the target sound in the initial position. Say the phrase for each picture as many times as indicated.

In Class: _____   Homework: _____

A rabbit on a raft.

A rabbit on a robot.

A rabbit on a radio.

A rabbit on a rattle.

A rabbit on a rope.

A rabbit on a raincoat.

A rabbit on a raccoon.

A rabbit on a rock.

A rabbit on a rake.

A rabbit in the rain.

A rabbit on a rocket.

A rabbit on a road.

Great Ideas for Teaching, Inc.   r-1   ARTICULATION DRILL SKILLS

Name: _____ r

The purpose of this activity is to provide repetitious practice of the target sound in the initial position. Say the phrase for each picture as many times as indicated.

In Class: _____   Homework: _____

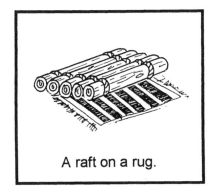
A raft on a rug.

A robot on a rug.

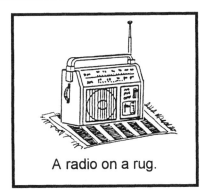
A radio on a rug.

A rattle on a rug.

A rope on a rug.

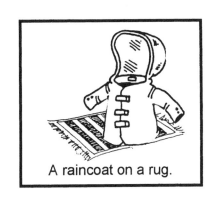
A raincoat on a rug.

A raccoon on a rug.

A rock on a rug.

A rake on a rug.

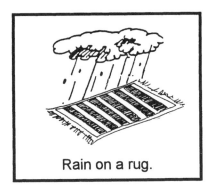
Rain on a rug.

A rocket on a rug.

A road on a rug.

Great Ideas for Teaching, Inc.   r-2   ARTICULATION DRILL SKILLS

Name: _____ r

The purpose of this activity is to provide repetitious practice of the target sound in the initial position. Say the phrase for each picture as many times as indicated.

In Class: _____ Homework: _____

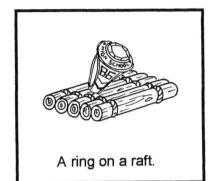
A ring on a raft.

A ring on a robot.

A ring on a radio.

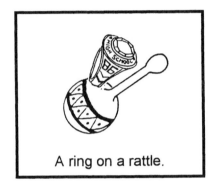
A ring on a rattle.

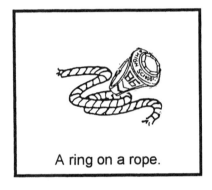
A ring on a rope.

A ring on a raincoat.

A ring on a raccoon.

A ring on a rock.

A ring on a rake.

A ring in the rain.

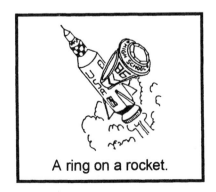
A ring on a rocket.

A ring on a road.

Great Ideas for Teaching, Inc.   r-3   ARTICULATION DRILL SKILLS

Name: _____ r

The purpose of this activity is to provide repetitious practice of the target sound in the initial and medial positions. Say the phrase for each picture as many times as indicated.

In Class: _____ Homework: _____

A carrot on a raft.

A carrot on a robot.

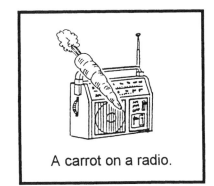
A carrot on a radio.

A carrot on a rattle.

A carrot on a rope.

A carrot on a raincoat.

A carrot on a raccoon.

A carrot on a rock.

A carrot on a rake.

A carrot in the rain.

A carrot on a rocket.

A carrot on a road.

Great Ideas for Teaching, Inc.   r-4   ARTICULATION DRILL SKILLS

Name: _____ r

The purpose of this activity is to provide repetitious practice of the target sound in the initial and final positions. Say the phrase for each picture as many times as indicated.

In Class: _____ Homework: _____

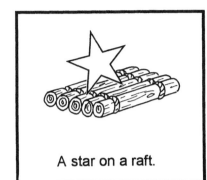
A star on a raft.

A star on a robot.

A star on a radio.

A star on a rattle.

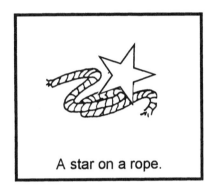
A star on a rope.

A star on a raincoat.

A star on a raccoon.

A star on a rock.

A star on a rake.

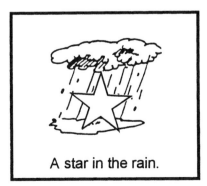
A star in the rain.

A star on a rocket.

A star on a road.

Great Ideas for Teaching, Inc. ARTICULATION DRILL SKILLS

Name: _____ S

The purpose of this activity is to provide repetitious practice of the target sound in the initial (and one final) position. Say the phrase for each picture as many times as indicated.

In Class: _____ Homework: _____

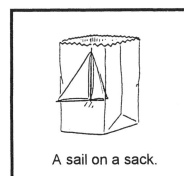
A sail on a sack.

A sail on soup.

A sail on the sun.

A sail on a sailor.

A sail on a safe.

A sail on a saw.

A sail on a seal.

A sail on a sandwich.

A sail on a seven.

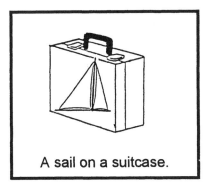
A sail on a suitcase.

A sail on a sock.

A sail on soap.

Great Ideas for Teaching, Inc.   s-1   ARTICULATION DRILL SKILLS

Name: _____ S

The purpose of this activity is to provide repetitious practice of the target sound in the initial (and one final) position. Say the phrase for each picture as many times as indicated.

In Class: _____   Homework: _____

A seal on a sack.

A seal on soup.

A seal on the sun.

A seal on a sailor.

A seal on a safe.

A seal on a saw.

A seal on a seal.

A seal on a sandwich.

A seal on a seven.

A seal on a suitcase.

A seal on a sock.

A seal on soap.

Great Ideas for Teaching, Inc.   ARTICULATION DRILL SKILLS

Name: _____ S

The purpose of this activity is to provide repetitious practice of the target sound in the initial and final positions. Say the phrase for each picture as many times as indicated.

In Class: _____ Homework: _____

A six on a sack.

A six on soup.

A six on the sun.

A six on a sailor.

A six on a safe.

A six on a saw.

A six on a seal.

A six on a sandwich.

A six on a seven.

A six on a suitcase.

A six on a sock.

A six on soap.

Great Ideas for Teaching, Inc. ARTICULATION DRILL SKILLS

Name: _____ S

The purpose of this activity is to provide repetitious practice of the target sound in the initial, medial and final positions. Say the phrase for each picture as many times as indicated.

In Class: _____ Homework: _____

A blossom on a sack.

A blossom on soup.

A blossom on the sun.

A blossom on a sailor.

A blossom on a safe.

A blossom on a saw.

A blossom on a seal.

A blossom on a sandwich.

A blossom on a seven.

A blossom on a suitcase.

A blossom on a sock.

A blossom on soap.

Great Ideas for Teaching, Inc. ARTICULATION DRILL SKILLS

Name: _____ S

The purpose of this activity is to provide repetitious practice of the target sound in the initial and medial positions. Say the phrase for each picture as many times as indicated.

In Class: _____   Homework: _____

A seesaw on a sack.

A seesaw on soup.

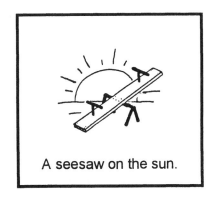
A seesaw on the sun.

A seesaw on a sailor.

A seesaw on a safe.

A seesaw on a saw.

A seesaw on a seal.

A seesaw on a sandwich.

A seesaw on a seven.

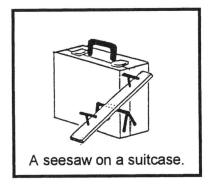
A seesaw on a suitcase.

A seesaw on a sock.

A seesaw on soap.

Great Ideas for Teaching, Inc.   s-5   ARTICULATION DRILL SKILLS

Name: _____   t

The purpose of this activity is to provide repetitious practice of the target sound in the initial position. Say the phrase for each picture as many times as indicated.

In Class: _____   Homework: _____

A tag on a table.

A tag on a tiger.

A tag on some toes.

A tag on a towel.

A tag on a top.

A tag on toys.

A tag on a turkey.

A tag on a tank.

A tag on a tie.

A tag on some tape.

A tag on a tire.

A tag on a tack.

Great Ideas for Teaching, Inc.　　t-1　　ARTICULATION DRILL SKILLS

Name: _____   t

The purpose of this activity is to provide repetitious practice of the target sound in the initial position. Say the phrase for each picture as many times as indicated.

In Class: _____   Homework: _____

A two on a table.

A two on a tiger.

A two on some toes.

A two on a towel.

A two on a top.

A two on toys.

A two on a turkey.

A two on a tank.

A two on a tie.

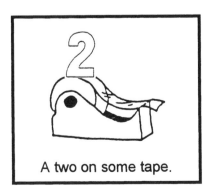
A two on some tape.

A two on a tire.

A two on a tack.

Great Ideas for Teaching, Inc.   ARTICULATION DRILL SKILLS

Name: _____ t

The purpose of this activity is to provide repetitious practice of the target sound in the initial position. Say the phrase for each picture as many times as indicated.

In Class: _____   Homework: _____

A "t" on a table.

A "t" on a tiger.

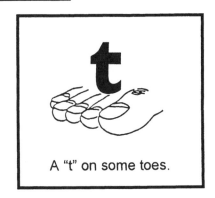
A "t" on some toes.

A "t" on a towel.

A "t" on a top.

A "t" on toys.

A "t" on a turkey.

A "t" on a tank.

A "t" on a tie.

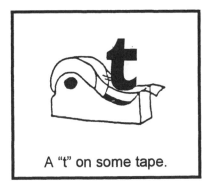
A "t" on some tape.

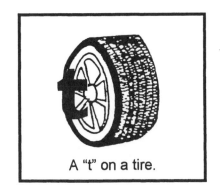
A "t" on a tire.

A "t" on a tack.

Great Ideas for Teaching, Inc.   t-3   ARTICULATION DRILL SKILLS

Name: _____ t

The purpose of this activity is to provide repetitious practice of the target sound in the initial and medial positions. Say the phrase for each picture as many times as indicated.

In Class: _____   Homework: _____

A button on a table.

A button on a tiger.

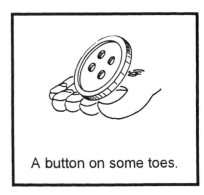
A button on some toes.

A button on a towel.

A button on a top.

A button on toys.

A button on a turkey.

A button on a tank.

A button on a tie.

A button on some tape.

A button on a tire.

A button on a tack.

Great Ideas for Teaching, Inc.   t-4   ARTICULATION DRILL SKILLS

Name: _____ t

The purpose of this activity is to provide repetitious practice of the target sound in the initial and final positions. Say the phrase for each picture as many times as indicated.

In Class: _____   Homework: _____

A bat on a table.

A bat on a tiger.

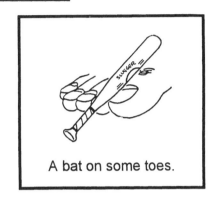
A bat on some toes.

A bat on a towel.

A bat on a top.

A bat on toys.

A bat on a turkey.

A bat on a tank.

A bat on a tie.

A bat on some tape.

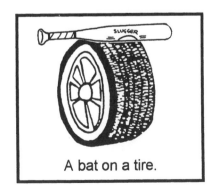
A bat on a tire.

A bat on a tack.

Great Ideas for Teaching, Inc.   t-5   ARTICULATION DRILL SKILLS

Name: _____ V

The purpose of this activity is to provide repetitious practice of the target sound in the initial position. Say the phrase for each picture as many times as indicated.

In Class: _____   Homework: _____

A "v" on a vampire.

A "v" on a van.

A "v" on a valentine box.

A "v" on a valentine.

A "v" on a vulture.

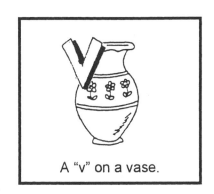
A "v" on a vase.

A "v" on a veil.

A "v" on a violin.

A "v" on a vine.

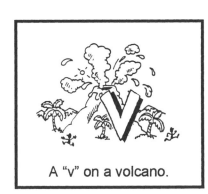
A "v" on a volcano.

A "v" on a vacuum.

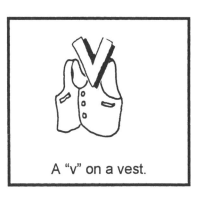
A "v" on a vest.

Great Ideas for Teaching, Inc.　　　　　ARTICULATION DRILL SKILLS

Name: _____ V

The purpose of this activity is to provide repetitious practice of the target sound in the initial position. Say the phrase for each picture as many times as indicated.

In Class: _____   Homework: _____

A valentine on a vampire.

A valentine on a van.

A valentine on a valentine box.

A valentine on a valentine.

A valentine on a vulture.

A valentine on a vase.

A valentine on a veil.

A valentine on a violin.

A valentine on a vine.

A valentine on a volcano.

A valentine on a vacuum.

A valentine on a vest.

Great Ideas for Teaching, Inc.   ARTICULATION DRILL SKILLS

Name: _____ V

The purpose of this activity is to provide repetitious practice of the target sound in the initial position. Say the phrase for each picture as many times as indicated.

In Class: _____   Homework: _____

A volleyball on a vampire.

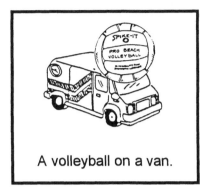
A volleyball on a van.

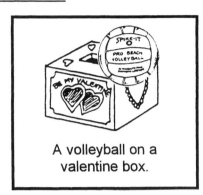
A volleyball on a valentine box.

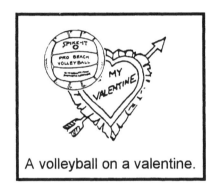
A volleyball on a valentine.

A volleyball on a vulture.

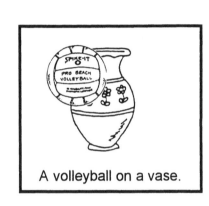
A volleyball on a vase.

A volleyball on a veil.

A volleyball on a violin.

A volleyball on a vine.

A volleyball on a volcano.

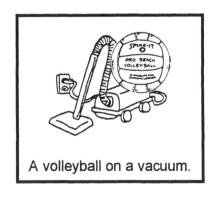
A volleyball on a vacuum.

A volleyball on a vest.

Great Ideas for Teaching, Inc.   v-3   ARTICULATION DRILL SKILLS

Name: _____ V

The purpose of this activity is to provide repetitious practice of the target sound in the initial and medial positions. Say the phrase for each picture as many times as indicated.

In Class: _____ Homework: _____

A seven on a vampire.

A seven on a van.

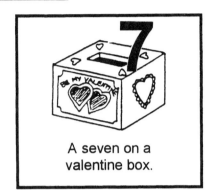
A seven on a valentine box.

A seven on a valentine.

A seven on a vulture.

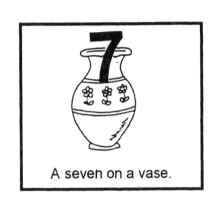
A seven on a vase.

A seven on a veil.

A seven on a violin.

A seven on a vine.

A seven on a volcano.

A seven on a vacuum.

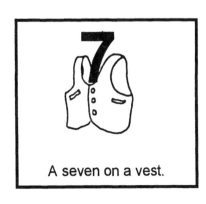
A seven on a vest.

Great Ideas for Teaching, Inc.　　　　　ARTICULATION DRILL SKILLS

Name: _____ V

The purpose of this activity is to provide repetitious practice of the target sound in the initial and final positions. Say the phrase for each picture as many times as indicated.

In Class: _____ Homework: _____

A five on a vampire.

A five on a van.

A five on a valentine box.

A five on a valentine.

A five on a vulture.

A five on a vase.

A five on a veil.

A five on a violin.

A five on a vine.

A five on a volcano.

A five on a vacuum.

A five on a vest.

Great Ideas for Teaching, Inc.   v-5   ARTICULATION DRILL SKILLS

Name: _____ **W**

The purpose of this activity is to provide repetitious practice of the target sound in the initial position. Say the phrase for each picture as many times as indicated.

In Class: _____   Homework: _____

A witch on a window.

A witch on a wastebasket.

A witch on a wig.

A witch on watermelon.

A witch on wood.

A witch on a windmill.

A witch on a web.

A witch on a walrus.

A witch on a watch.

A witch on a well.

A witch on a winking girl.

A witch on a wagon.

Great Ideas for Teaching, Inc.　　　　ARTICULATION DRILL SKILLS

Name: _____   **W**

The purpose of this activity is to provide repetitious practice of the target sound in the initial position. Say the phrase for each picture as many times as indicated.

In Class: _____   Homework: _____

A wand on a window.

A wand on a wastebasket.

A wand on a wig.

A wand on watermelon.

A wand on wood.

A wand on a windmill.

A wand on a web.

A wand on a walrus.

A wand on a watch.

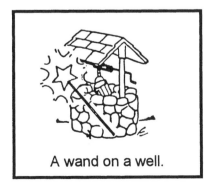
A wand on a well.

A wand on a winking girl.

A wand on a wagon.

Great Ideas for Teaching, Inc.   w-2   ARTICULATION DRILL SKILLS

Name: _____

W

The purpose of this activity is to provide repetitious practice of the target sound in the initial position. Say the phrase for each picture as many times as indicated.

In Class: _____   Homework: _____

Water on a window.

Water on a wastebasket.

Water on a wig.

Water on watermelon.

Water on wood.

Water on a windmill.

Water on a web.

Water on a walrus.

Water on a watch.

Water on a well.

Water on a winking girl.

Water on a wagon.

Great Ideas for Teaching, Inc.   ARTICULATION DRILL SKILLS

Name: _____ W

The purpose of this activity is to provide repetitious practice of the target sound in the initial and medial positions. Say the phrase for each picture as many times as indicated.

In Class: _____   Homework: _____

A sandwich on a window.

A sandwich on a wastebasket.

A sandwich on a wig.

A sandwich on watermelon.

A sandwich on wood.

A sandwich on a windmill.

A sandwich on a web.

A sandwich on a walrus.

A sandwich on a watch.

A sandwich on a well.

A sandwich on a winking girl.

A sandwich on a wagon.

Great Ideas for Teaching, Inc.   w-4   ARTICULATION DRILL SKILLS

Name: _____ W

The purpose of this activity is to provide repetitious practice of the target sound in the initial and medial positions. Say the phrase for each picture as many times as indicated.

In Class: _____   Homework: _____

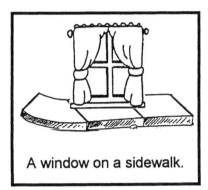
A window on a sidewalk.

A wastebasket on a sidewalk.

A wig on a sidewalk.

A watermelon on a sidewalk.

Wood on a sidewalk.

A windmill on a sidewalk.

A web on a sidewalk.

A walrus on a sidewalk.

A watch on a sidewalk.

A well on a sidewalk.

A winking girl on a sidewalk.

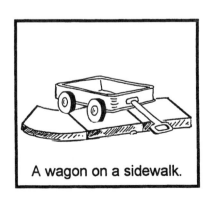
A wagon on a sidewalk.

Great Ideas for Teaching, Inc.   ARTICULATION DRILL SKILLS

Name: _____   Z

The purpose of this activity is to provide repetitious practice of the target sound in the initial, medial and final positions. Say the phrase for each picture as many times as indicated.

In Class: _____   Homework: _____

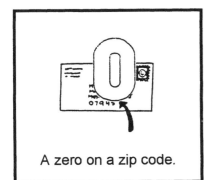
A zero on a zip code.

A zero on a zebra.

A zero on a zipper.

A zero on a zigzag.

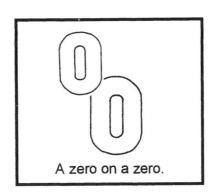
A zero on a zero.

A zero on zoo keepers.

A zero on a "z" puzzle.

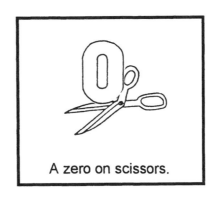
A zero on scissors.

A zero on a buzzer.

A zero on keys.

A zero on bees.

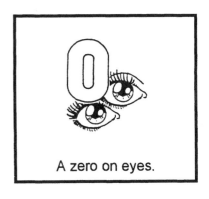
A zero on eyes.

Great Ideas for Teaching, Inc.   z-1   ARTICULATION DRILL SKILLS

Name: _____ Z

The purpose of this activity is to provide repetitious practice of the target sound in the initial, medial and final positions. Say the phrase for each picture as many times as indicated.

In Class: _____   Homework: _____

A "z" on a zip code.

A "z" on a zebra.

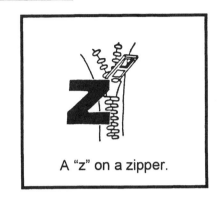
A "z" on a zipper.

A "z" on a zigzag.

A "z" on a zero.

A "z" on zoo keepers.

A "z" on a "z" puzzle.

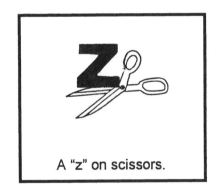
A "z" on scissors.

A "z" on a buzzer.

A "z" on keys.

A "z" on bees.

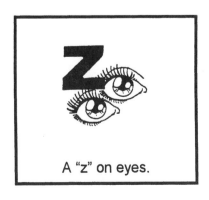
A "z" on eyes.

Great Ideas for Teaching, Inc.   ARTICULATION DRILL SKILLS

Name: _____ Z

The purpose of this activity is to provide repetitious practice of the target sound in the initial, medial and final positions. Say the phrase for each picture as many times as indicated.

In Class: _____ Homework: _____

A rose on a zip code.

A rose on a zebra.

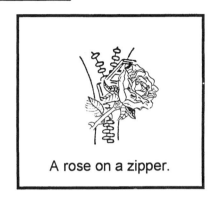
A rose on a zipper.

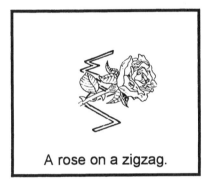
A rose on a zigzag.

A rose on a zero.

A rose on zoo keepers.

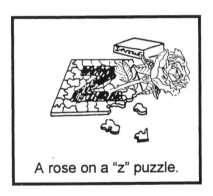
A rose on a "z" puzzle.

A rose on scissors.

A rose on a buzzer.

A rose on keys.

A rose on bees.

A rose on eyes.

Great Ideas for Teaching, Inc.   z-3   ARTICULATION DRILL SKILLS

Name: _____ Z

The purpose of this activity is to provide repetitious practice of the target sound in the initial, medial and final positions. Say the phrase for each picture as many times as indicated.

In Class: _____   Homework: _____

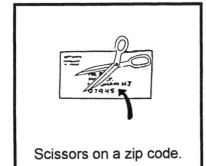
Scissors on a zip code.

Scissors on a zebra.

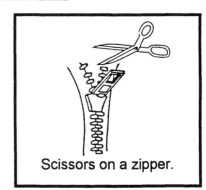
Scissors on a zipper.

Scissors on a zigzag.

Scissors on a zero.

Scissors on zoo keepers.

Scissors on a "z" puzzle.

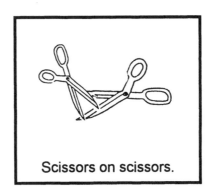
Scissors on scissors.

Scissors on a buzzer.

Scissors on keys.

Scissors on bees.

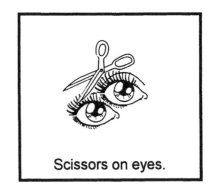
Scissors on eyes.

Name: _____ Z

The purpose of this activity is to provide repetitious practice of the target sound in the initial, medial and final positions. Say the phrase for each picture as many times as indicated.

In Class: _____   Homework: _____

Cheese on a zip code.

Cheese on a zebra.

Cheese on a zipper.

Cheese on a zigzag.

Cheese on a zero.

Cheese on zoo keepers.

Cheese on a "z" puzzle.

Cheese on scissors.

Cheese on a buzzer.

Cheese on keys.

Cheese on bees.

Cheese on eyes.

Great Ideas for Teaching, Inc.   z-5   ARTICULATION DRILL SKILLS

Name: _____   ch

The purpose of this activity is to provide repetitious practice of the target sound in the initial (and one final) position. Say the phrase for each picture as many times as indicated.

In Class: _____   Homework: _____

A chicken on a chimney.

A chicken on cheese.

A chicken on a chain.

A chicken on chicks.

A chicken on a checkmark.

A chicken on a chest.

A chicken on chalk.

A chicken on children.

A chicken on a cheesecake.

A chicken on a chicken leg.

A chicken on a church.

A chicken on a chair.

Great Ideas for Teaching, Inc.   ch-1   ARTICULATION DRILL SKILLS

Name: _____ ch

The purpose of this activity is to provide repetitious practice of the target sound in the initial (and one final) position. Say the phrase for each picture as many times as indicated.

In Class: _____ Homework: _____

A chipmunk on a chimney.

A chipmunk on cheese.

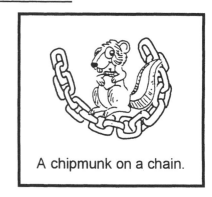
A chipmunk on a chain.

A chipmunk on chicks.

A chipmunk on a checkmark.

A chipmunk on a chest.

A chipmunk on chalk.

A chipmunk on children.

A chimpmunk on a cheesecake.

A chipmunk on a chicken leg.

A chipmunk on a church.

A chipmunk on a chair.

Great Ideas for Teaching, Inc.   ARTICULATION DRILL SKILLS

Name: _____ ch

The purpose of this activity is to provide repetitious practice of the target sound in the initial (and one final) position. Say the phrase for each picture as many times as indicated.

In Class: _____ Homework: _____

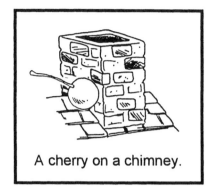
A cherry on a chimney.

A cherry on cheese.

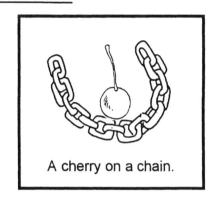
A cherry on a chain.

A cherry on chicks.

A cherry on a checkmark.

A cherry on a chest.

A cherry on chalk.

A cherry on children.

A cherry on a cheesecake.

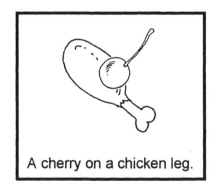
A cherry on a chicken leg.

A cherry on a church.

A cherry on a chair.

Great Ideas for Teaching, Inc.   ch-3   ARTICULATION DRILL SKILLS

Name: _____ ch

The purpose of this activity is to provide repetitious practice of the target sound in the initial, medial and final positions. Say the phrase for each picture as many times as indicated.

In Class: _____ Homework: _____

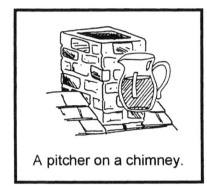
A pitcher on a chimney.

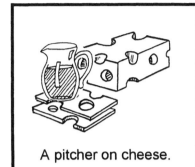
A pitcher on cheese.

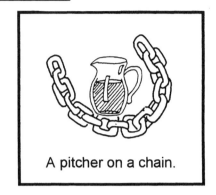
A pitcher on a chain.

A pitcher on chicks.

A pitcher on a checkmark.

A pitcher on a chest.

A pitcher on chalk.

A pitcher on children.

A pitcher on a cheesecake.

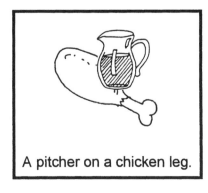
A pitcher on a chicken leg.

A pitcher on a church.

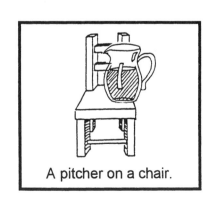
A pitcher on a chair.

Great Ideas for Teaching, Inc.   ch-4   ARTICULATION DRILL SKILLS

Name: _____ **ch**

The purpose of this activity is to provide repetitious practice of the target sound in the initial and final positions. Say the phrase for each picture as many times as indicated.

In Class: _____ Homework: _____

A witch on a chimney.

A witch on cheese.

A witch on a chain.

A witch on chicks.

A witch on a checkmark.

A witch on a chest.

A witch on chalk.

A witch on children.

A witch on a cheesecake.

A witch on a chicken leg.

A witch on a church.

A witch on a chair.

Great Ideas for Teaching, Inc. ch-5 ARTICULATION DRILL SKILLS

Name: _____ sh

The purpose of this activity is to provide repetitious practice of the target sound in the initial position. Say the phrase for each picture as many times as indicated.

In Class: _____ Homework: _____

A shoe on a shutter.

A shoe on a shoe.

A shoe on a ship.

A shoe on a sheriff.

A shoe on a shelf.

A shoe on a shower.

A shoe on sugar.

A shoe on a shield.

A shoe on a shamrock.

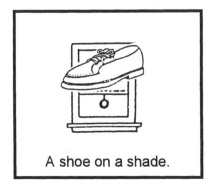
A shoe on a shade.

A shoe on a shadow.

A shoe on a shirt.

Great Ideas for Teaching, Inc.   sh-1   ARTICULATION DRILL SKILLS

Name: _____ sh

The purpose of this activity is to provide repetitious practice of the target sound in the initial position. Say the phrase for each picture as many times as indicated.

In Class: _____   Homework: _____

A shell on a shutter.

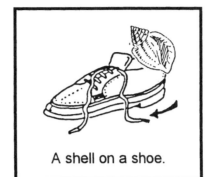
A shell on a shoe.

A shell on a ship.

A shell on a sheriff.

A shell on a shelf.

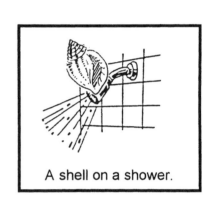
A shell on a shower.

A shell on sugar.

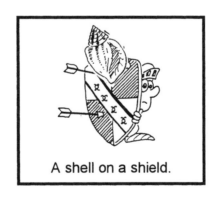
A shell on a shield.

A shell on a shamrock.

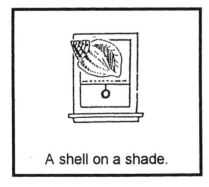
A shell on a shade.

A shell on a shadow.

A shell on a shirt.

Great Ideas for Teaching, Inc.   ARTICULATION DRILL SKILLS

Name: _____ sh

The purpose of this activity is to provide repetitious practice of the target sound in the initial position. Say the phrase for each picture as many times as indicated.

In Class: _____   Homework: _____

A sheep on a shutter.

A sheep on a shoe.

A sheep on a ship.

A sheep on a sheriff.

A sheep on a shelf.

A sheep on a shower.

A sheep on sugar.

A sheep on a shield.

A sheep on a shamrock.

A sheep on a shade.

A sheep on a shadow.

A sheep on a shirt.

Great Ideas for Teaching, Inc.   sh-3   ARTICULATION DRILL SKILLS

Name: _____ sh

The purpose of this activity is to provide repetitious practice of the target sound in the initial and medial positions. Say the phrase for each picture as many times as indicated.

In Class: _____   Homework: _____

A flashlight on a shutter.

A flashlight on a shoe.

A flashlight on a ship.

A flashlight on a sheriff.

A flashlight on a shelf.

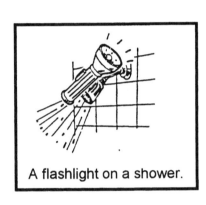
A flashlight on a shower.

A flashlight on sugar.

A flashlight on a shield.

A flashlight on a shamrock.

A flashlight on a shade.

A flashlight on a shadow.

A flashlight on a shirt.

Great Ideas for Teaching, Inc.   sh-4   ARTICULATION DRILL SKILLS

Name: _____ sh

The purpose of this activity is to provide repetitious practice of the target sound in the initial and final positions. Say the phrase for each picture as many times as indicated.

In Class: _____ Homework: _____

A fish on a shutter.

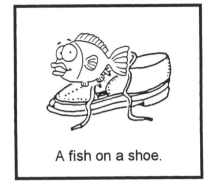
A fish on a shoe.

A fish on a ship.

A fish on a sheriff.

A fish on a shelf.

A fish on a shower.

A fish on sugar.

A fish on a shield.

A fish on a shamrock.

A fish on a shade.

A fish on a shadow.

A fish on a shirt.

Great Ideas for Teaching, Inc. sh-5 ARTICULATION DRILL SKILLS

Name: _____ **th**

The purpose of this activity is to provide repetitious practice of the target sound in the initial, medial and final positions. Say the phrase for each picture as many times as indicated.

In Class: _____   Homework: _____

A thumb on a thank-you note.

A thumb on a throat.

A thumb on a thirteen.

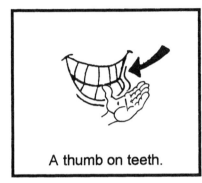
A thumb on teeth.

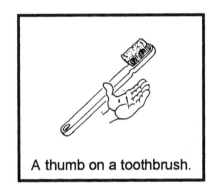
A thumb on a toothbrush.

A thumb on a thumbtack.

A thumb on a thermos.

A thumb on a thimble.

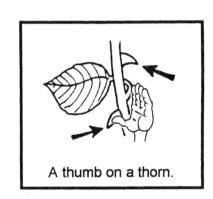
A thumb on a thorn.

A thumb on thread.

A thumb on a throne.

A thumb at Thanksgiving.

Great Ideas for Teaching, Inc.　　　th-1　　　ARTICULATION DRILL SKILLS

Name: _____ th

The purpose of this activity is to provide repetitious practice of the target sound in the initial, medial and final positions. Say the phrase for each picture as many times as indicated.

In Class: _____ Homework: _____

A three on a thank-you note.

A three on a throat.

A three on a thirteen.

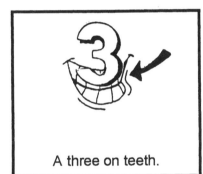
A three on teeth.

A three on a toothbrush.

A three on a thumbtack.

A three on a thermos.

A three on a thimble.

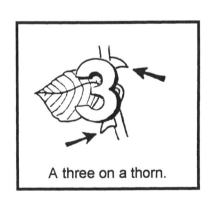
A three on a thorn.

A three on thread.

A three on a throne.

A three at Thanksgiving.

Great Ideas for Teaching, Inc. th-2 ARTICULATION DRILL SKILLS

Name: _____ th

The purpose of this activity is to provide repetitious practice of the target sound in the initial, medial and final positions. Say the phrase for each picture as many times as indicated.

In Class: _____ Homework: _____

A thimble on a thank-you note.

A thimble on a throat.

A thimble on a thirteen.

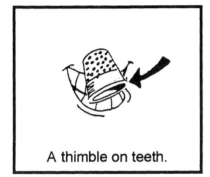
A thimble on teeth.

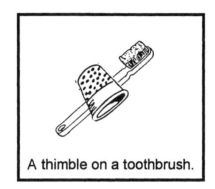
A thimble on a toothbrush.

A thimble on a thumbtack.

A thimble on a thermos.

A thimble on a thimble.

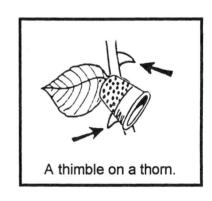
A thimble on a thorn.

A thimble on thread.

A thimble on a throne.

A thimble at Thanksgiving.

Great Ideas for Teaching, Inc. ARTICULATION DRILL SKILLS

Name: _____ th

The purpose of this activity is to provide repetitious practice of the target sound in the initial, medial and final positions. Say the phrase for each picture as many times as indicated.

In Class: _____   Homework: _____

Teeth on a thank-you note.

Teeth on a throat.

Teeth on a thirteen.

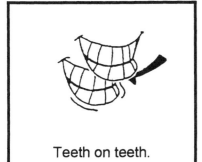
Teeth on teeth.

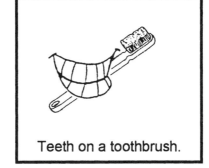
Teeth on a toothbrush.

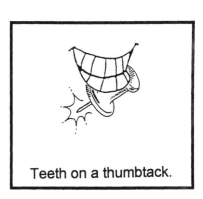
Teeth on a thumbtack.

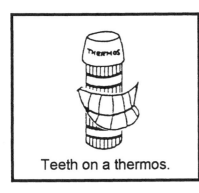
Teeth on a thermos.

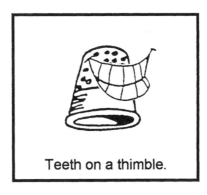
Teeth on a thimble.

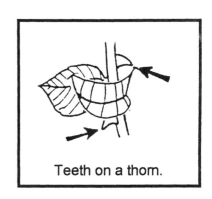
Teeth on a thorn.

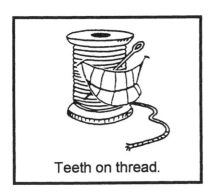
Teeth on thread.

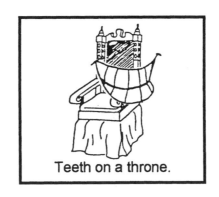
Teeth on a throne.

Teeth at Thanksgiving.

Great Ideas for Teaching, Inc.   th-4   ARTICULATION DRILL SKILLS

Name: _____

The purpose of this activity is to provide repetitious practice of the target sound in the initial, medial and final positions. Say the phrase for each picture as many times as indicated.

In Class: _____ Homework: _____

A birdbath on a thank-you note.

A birdbath on a throat.

A birdbath on a thirteen.

A birdbath on teeth.

A birdbath on a toothbrush.

A birdbath on a thumbtack.

A birdbath on a thermos.

A birdbath on a thimble.

A birdbath on a thorn.

A birdbath on thread.

A birdbath on a throne.

A birdbath at Thanksgiving.

Great Ideas for Teaching, Inc. ARTICULATION DRILL SKILLS